Search and Find
Space

Licensed exclusively to Top That Publishing Ltd
Tide Mill Way, Woodbridge, Suffolk, IP12 1AP, UK
www.topthatpublishing.com
Copyright © 2017 Tide Mill Media
All rights reserved
2 4 6 8 9 7 5 3 1
Manufactured in China

1 moon

2 explosions

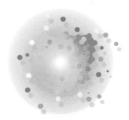

3 traffic controllers

4 guards

5 aliens with green heads

Control centre chaos

At the spaceflight control centre they are busy monitoring the intergalactic scene. Can you find all the things listed?

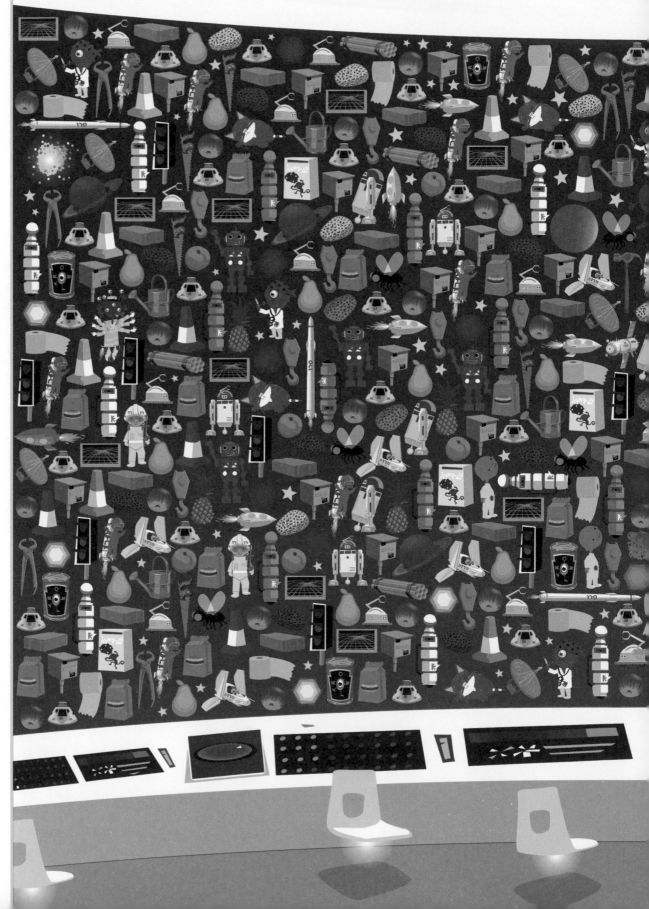

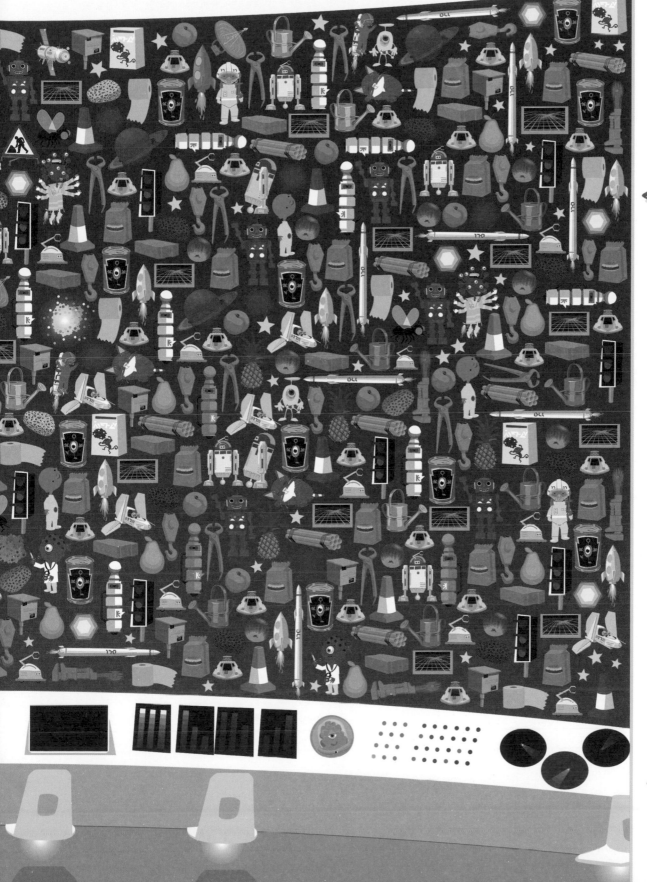

Can you find?

6 planets

7 space cats

8 cereal boxes

9 traffic cones

10 spaceships

Can you find?

1 receiver dish

2 alien spaceships

3 aliens with jetpacks

4 orange planets

5 planets with rings

Observation deck

The view from the observation deck is out of this world – literally! Can you find all the things listed?

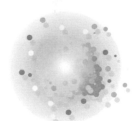

1 pink robot

2 red lights

3 oranges

4 pineapples

5 grabber cranes

The loading bay

The loading bay at the space station is a busy place. There's always someone (or something) coming and going! Can you find all the things listed?

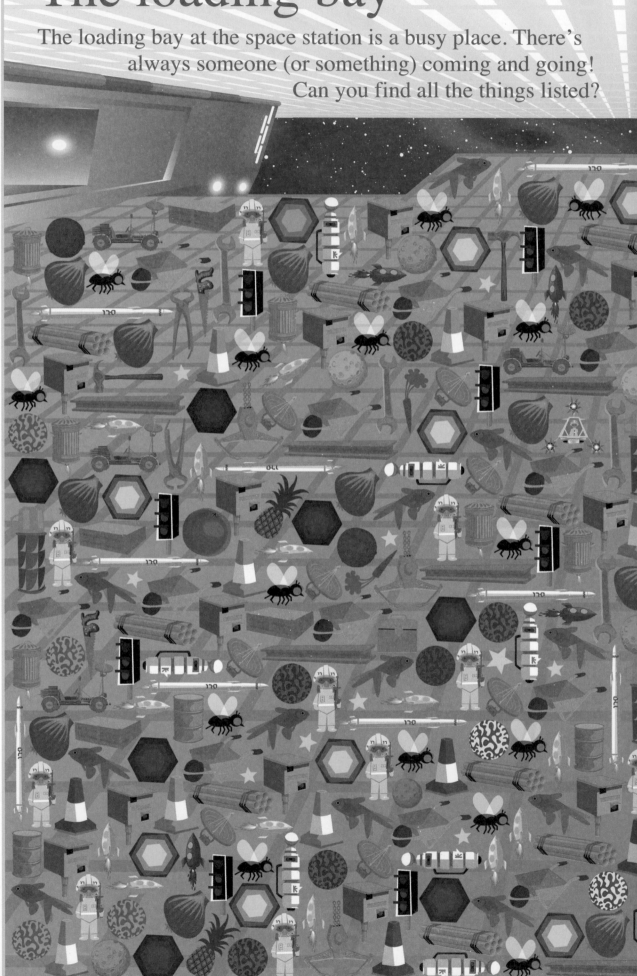

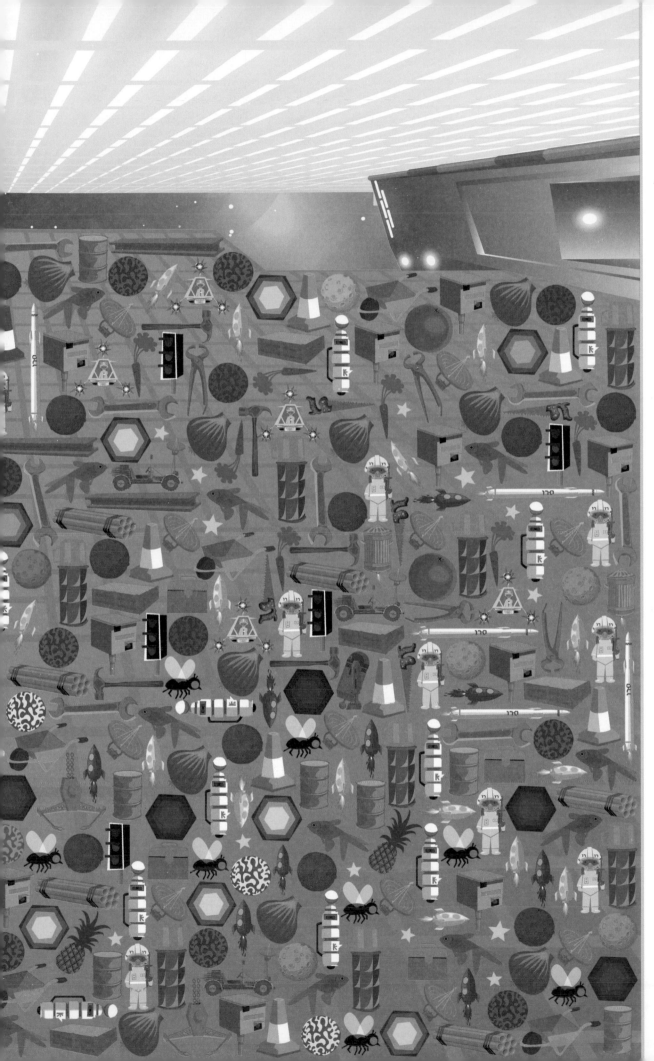

Can you find?

1 yellow car

2 fires

3 tanks

4 flags

5 explosions

Alien attack!

Uh-oh! Aliens have travelled to Earth and have started to attack! Can you find all the things listed?

Can you find?

6 helicopters

7 alien spacecraft

8 seagulls

9 soldiers like this

10 manholes

Scramble interceptors

Alien spacecraft are approaching the space station and the space station interceptor craft have been scrambled. Can you find all the things listed?

Can you find?

1 moon

2 red robots

3 grabber cranes

4 green robots

5 pink robots

Can you find?

6 barrels

7 crew with
red helmets

8 spaceships

9 crew with
blue helmets

10 crew with
green helmets

1 moon

2 planets

3 space dragons

4 blue spacecraft

5 missiles

Look out!

As the space station pilots intercept the approaching craft, the aliens unleash all of their firepower! Can you find all the things listed?

6 interceptor craft

7 alien craft like this

8 explosions

9 asteroids

10 rocket bins

1 furry alien

2 yellow robots

3 black starships

4 blue robots

5 space flies

Salute the heroes

The alien invaders have been defeated! As the triumphant interceptor pilots return to the space station, people line the viewing decks to congratulate them. Can you find all the things listed?

Can you find?

6 red spaceships

7 yellow spaceships

8 satellites

9 blue spaceships

10 missiles

Can you find?

1 silly alien

2 rocket trailers

3 alien dogs

4 space harvesters

5 flying saucers

Planet Yoobee

Planet Yoobee is home to little green men who grow crops to make their favourite food – breakfast cereal! Can you find all the things listed below?

Can you find?

6 jars of alien eyes

7 red cereal boxes

8 yellow cereal boxes

9 turtle-toucans

10 allen farmers

Space race

It's the annual intergalactic pod racing championship.
Some of the fastest craft ever built are racing today.
Can you find all the things listed?

Can you find?

1 broken down pod

2 purple dragons

3 blue cereal boxes

4 aliens like this

5 flying saucers

Giant biospheres

The space station is completely self-sufficient. Fruit, vegetables and other crops are grown in giant biospheres. Can you find all the things listed?

Can you find?

1 watermelon

2 watering cans

3 scientists

4 bunches of bananas

5 tanks of carrots

Can you find?

1 blue alien

2 drones

3 green bottles

4 moon buggies

5 red aliens

Explorers

Space scientists search the galaxy looking for new planets that can sustain human life. Can you find all the things listed?

Can you find?

6 guards

7 purple
bottles

8 green
robots

9 space
rovers

10 red lights

1 pink planet

2 signs like this

3 aliens like this

4 traffic cones

5 orange rockets

Space mall

With its trendy shops and restaurants, this is probably the coolest shopping spot in the galaxy! Can you find all the things listed?

Can you find?

6 space takeaways

7 milkshakes

8 blue rockets

9 flying saucers

10 drones

Can you find?

1 hammer

2 flasks

3 rocket bins

4 crane hooks

5 gun turrets

Repair dock

Spaceships need constant repair and updating. This vast hangar is being used to make modifications to a destroyer vessel. Can you find all the things listed?

Can you find?

6 crates of space cargo

7 adjustable spanners

8 barrels

9 work lamps

10 mechanics

Can you find?

1 satellite

2 speed cameras

3 traffic controllers

4 craft like this

5 traffic lights

Flying test

All children who live on board the space station must learn to fly small two-seater spaceships by the time they are ten years old. Can you find all the things listed?

Can you find?

6 drones

7 alien spaceships

8 pineapples

9 astcroids

10 two-seater spaceships

Can you find?

1 frying pan

2 caravans

3 torches

4 blue coolers

5 tents

Visit to Earth

This alien spaceship has paid a visit to Earth. The aliens are beaming up a child to see if he wants to watch a movie. Can you find all the things listed?

Can you find?

6 camping chairs

7 pairs of pants

8 cans of beans

9 toilet rolls

10 buckets

Spacewalk search

While travelling close to an unknown planet,
this starship was damaged by passing asteroids.
It's the crew's job to repair the damage.
Can you find all the things listed?

Can you find?

1 flask

2 toolboxes

3 forks

4 people at
work signs

5 hammers

Can you find?

6 yellow spacecraft

7 toilet rolls

8 explosions

9 wheeled robots

10 traffic cones

Can you find?

**1 guard
like this**

**2 jetpack
pilots**

**3 yellow
traffic cones**

**4 moon
buggies**

**5 blue
wheeled
robots**

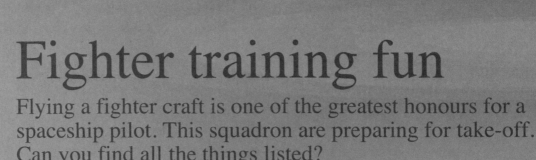

Fighter training fun

Flying a fighter craft is one of the greatest honours for a
spaceship pilot. This squadron are preparing for take-off.
Can you find all the things listed?

Can you find?

6 blue guards

7 red robots

8 milkshakes

9 drones

10 red pilots

Can you find?

1 melting moon

2 black spaceships

3 beach balls

4 one-eyed sun visors

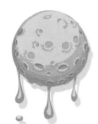

5 parasols

Hot, hot, hot!

This planet is scorchingly close to its sun and the temperature is nearly 600°C! Can you find all the things listed?

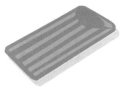

Can you find?

1 governor's portrait

2 space cats

3 furry aliens

4 red aliens

5 aliens with claws

Alien escape

Uh-oh! All kinds of the worst, most troublesome aliens have escaped from the space station prison. Can you find all the things listed?

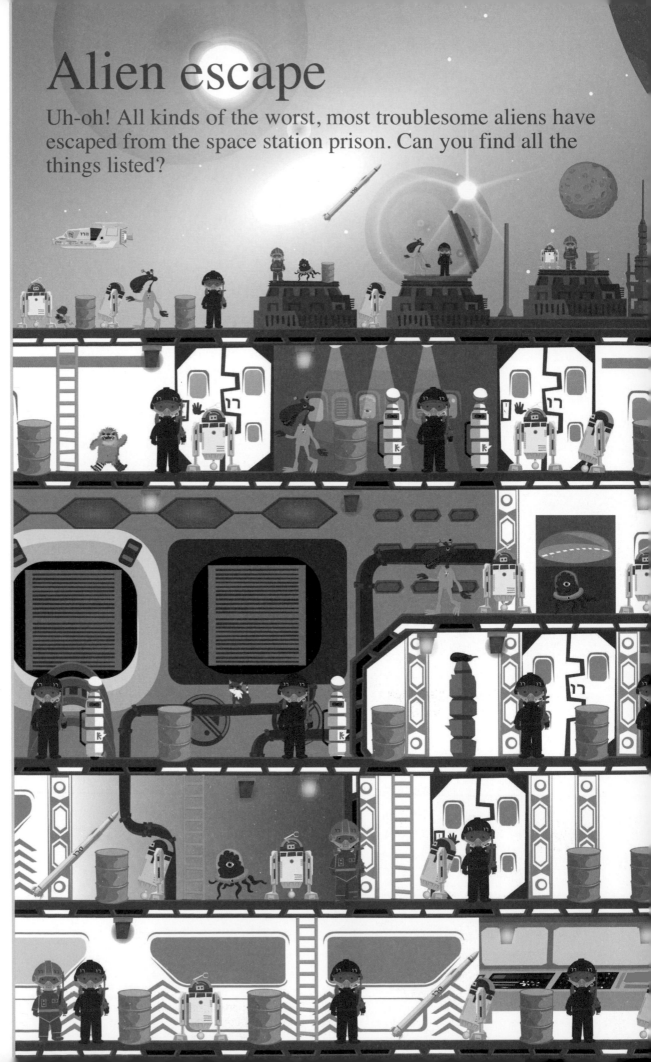

Alien lessons

It's time for school for these young aliens, but some of them are not behaving! Can you find all the things listed?

Can you find?

1 tuba

2 spacecraft

3 Venus flytraps

4 tablet computers

5 space crabs

Can you find?

6 balls of paper

7 open books

8 paper aeroplanes

9 flowerpots

10 marbles

Can you find?

1 orange planet

2 two-headed snakes

3 helicopters

4 cranes

5 aeroplanes

Alien cousins

This planet is the most similar to Earth and the aliens who live here are suspiciously like human beings. But something's not quite right! Can you find all the things listed?

Can you find?

6 briefcases

7 crisp packets

8 firemen

9 milkshakes

10 pineapples

Can you find?

1
Stegosaurus

2
Diplodocus

3
Allosaurus

4
Triceratops

5 alien
spacccraft

Dinosaurs in space

Although dinosaurs became extinct on Earth millions of years
ago, on this planet they are still alive and well. Can you find
all the things listed?

6 moon buggies

7 drones

8 Pterodactyls

9 Coelophysis

10 Iguanodon

Alien sickbay

At this space hospital, the doctors never know what kind of problem they'll see, or even what species! Can you find all the things listed?

Can you find?

1 spaceship

2 brown mugs

3 red aliens

4 pairs of crutches

5 weird green sponges

Can you find?

1 spaceship like this

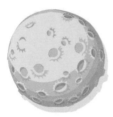

2 yellow moons

3 green robots

4 spaceships like this

5 miners with scanners

Mine craft

The natural resources on Earth ran out long ago. This mining craft searches the universe for precious metals and minerals. Can you find all the things listed?